A Dog's Little Instruction Book

Other Little Instruction Books

A Cat's Little Instruction Book
by Leigh W. Rutledge

Life's Little Instruction Book
Life's Little Instruction Book II
by H. Jackson Brown Jr

A Baby's Little Instruction Book
A Pig's Little Instruction Book
A Teddy Bear's Little Instruction Book
by David Brawn

A Dog's Little Instruction Book

David Brawn

HarperCollins*Publishers*

HarperCollins*Publishers*
77–85 Fulham Palace Road,
Hammersmith, London W6 8JB

www.**fire**and**water**.com

First published by Thorsons 1994
Published by HarperCollins*Publishers* 1999

3 5 7 9 10 8 6 4 2

© David Brawn 1994

David Brawn asserts the moral right
to be identified as the author of this work

Illustrations by Wendy Jones

A catalogue record for this book
is available from the British Library

ISBN 0 7225 3908 8

Printed and bound in Great Britain by
Martins the Printers Ltd, Berwick upon Tweed

Author's Note

Do not let your dog read this book.
Instinct will have equipped him with
most of its contents, and it is probably
wise not to teach him any of the
remaining pieces of advice which,
through selective breeding, it has taken
mankind centuries to remove.
You have been warned.

In memory of Sam
– there's no one quite like your first dog

- Treat teddy bears with the contempt they deserve

- Learn to beg properly

- Pretend you can't hear a silent dog whistle

Newspapers spread on the floor are not for reading

Don't eat vegetables – they give you wind

Never take a doggie chocolate in preference to the real thing

Stick a cold nose up a visitor's dress

Caged rodents are a snack waiting for the tin opener

Never eat your meal if you suspect it has a tablet in it

Don't mess with hedgehogs

Get to know your local police dog – you don't know when you'll need him

Don't chase traffic

- Prove to people you're not colour-blind

- Sleep in a thoroughfare

- Attack the vacuum cleaner, but be wary of the lawnmower

- Never use a dog loo

- Learn to pull chocolates off Christmas trees

- Leave nose marks on clean windows

- Be respectful towards corgis

Never be seen in tartan

Don't inhale talcum powder

Avoid fizzy drinks

Don't attempt to crack open the tortoise

- Don't countenance incest

- Eat flies, but not wasps

- Don't let people blame you when *they* fart

- Don't go to sleep on ants' nests

Hold a grudge against T.S. Eliot and Andrew Lloyd Webber

Pose for photographs, especially when you're not supposed to be in them

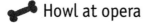 Howl at opera

Ask to be let out during a good film on TV

Pinch embarrassing rubbish from waste bins

Be hygienic – don't lick yourself after licking someone's face

Only swim in dirty water

Watch sheepdog trials on television

Don't eat a hot dog on principle

- Get in the way

- Drink from a birdbath in preference to a dog bowl

- Chase squirrels

Never look behind a television set when a racing car drives off the screen

Bark at night

Never take 'no' for an answer

- Avoid marking your territory on a prickly bush

- Always do the sort of turds pooper scoopers are not designed to cope with

Don't bite the hand that feeds you

Bark in noise abatement areas

Steer clear of broken glass

- Accidentally walk on wet concrete

- Never turn your back on a child with a water pistol

- Clean between your toes

- Never get dressed up to appear on novelty postcards

- Leap on someone who's reading a large newspaper

- Learn to distinguish between your doorbell and one on the television

- Don't leave the table until you've been given something to eat

- Don't be intimidated by larger breeds

- Start a trend – yawn

- Remember where you buried your bone

- Ignore evolution and find a better way to greet other dogs

- Don't crow about having private health insurance

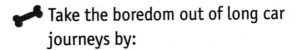 Take the boredom out of long car journeys by:

a) being sick
b) barking at cyclists
c) nose-printing on the windows

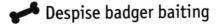 Despise badger baiting

Be the leader of the pack

Live up to being 'man's best friend'

Hide in the undergrowth where humans fear to tread

Control your jealousy

Don't wet yourself when having your tummy tickled

When you get old, learn some new tricks

- Try being friendly with the neighbour's dog

- Wear your muzzle with pride

- Hide when it thunders

- Pick up as many grass seeds in your coat as you can

Fight with the broom

Beware the vet with the thermometer

Play hide and seek

Recognize when your owners are going on holiday

- Only chew squeaky toys in company

- Never play with a squeaky toy that's been de-squeaked

- Have phantom pregnancies

- Be a tug of war champion

- Don't let neutering turn you into a shy, retiring fattie

- Never eat manure, even if you've been told that it's good for you

- Don't flash at the vicar

- Don't steal food from dustbins

- Take your vitamins

- If it's hot, lie down in cold water

Don't be too possessive – it's unlikely that anyone *will* want to steal your bone

Use shampoo *and* conditioner

Don't bite your nails

- Don't take the blame for the cat's misdemeanours

- Only drag your bottom on plush carpet

- Always have an alibi

Never chase a stuffed hare

Don't pick a fight with a pit bull terrier (unless you are one)

Ensure Father Christmas doesn't miss you out

Bring comfort by visiting old people

Be someone's hero

Take your owners for walks

Learn to find your own way home

Learn to say sorry

- Don't eat off a plate someone might have licked

- Do Sphinx impressions

- Never forget your wolverine ancestry, even if you're a chihuahua

- Aspire to be Top Dog

- Don't chew chair and table legs

- Push your nose under someone's elbow if you want attention

- Don't gnaw on chicken bones

- Never drink from a bowl with CAT on it

- Never trust someone who calls you 'dog' rather than by your name

If you live with another dog, don't rely on any leftover food still being there when you get back

Don't get depressed at Roadrunner

Take your master his slippers – don't chew them up

Don't agree to an 'arranged marriage' unless you really like each other

Have a large kennel, but resist ever going in it

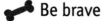 Be brave

Keep your tail away from
young children

Be inquisitive

- Be a doggone nuisance

- Go to obedience classes

- Crap on the beach

Refrain from cocking your leg up the Christmas tree

Learn to recognize the word for 'dog' in five languages

- Don't step on people's feet

- Cultivate a sad expression

- Children will love you if you play ball with them – until you puncture it

- Don't eat hot food

Don't chew a biro

Don't take sides in domestic disputes

Get into bed on a Sunday morning

Don't snore

Be loyal and obedient – when it suits you

Be carried on escalators

Look dejected when left outside shops and someone might give you something

Make it as difficult as possible to be lifted on to the vet's table

Don't be worried if your master shouts – his bark is worse than his bite

Don't mistake an early dinner for a between-meal snack

Teach your offspring that puppies should be heard and not seen

Don't be a gundog if you hate:

a) loud noises
b) the outdoors
c) the sight of blood

Don't be tempted to have a flutter on the greyhounds

Never underestimate the firepower of bad breath

Ponder over the origin of the phrase 'dog-eared'

No matter how revolting your meal, always ask for more

- Pose by an old gramophone

- Eat the sausage at retrieval classes

- Shake any towels that are coming to dry you to ensure they're properly dead

Don't drink seawater

Don't bark at a dog in the mirror or you'll give yourself a nasty fright

Don't cock your leg up an electric fence

Don't bark through a closed window at something that's too far away to hear it

If you do have to take a bath, remember the soap is for shampooing, not eating

- Don't tease a bigger dog for being tied up before checking he's not on an extending leash

- Never eat slug pellets (or slugs)

- Learn to snigger like Muttley

- Always sleep on a freshly-made bed in preference to an unmade one

- Know the sound of the fridge door

- Get your vaccinations

- Learn to unwrap your own presents

- Stick your head out the window of a fast-moving car (or preferably the sunroof)

- Don't chase sheep unless you're qualified

- Find out where to buy Scooby Snacks

- Stay indoors for fireworks

- Don't let the arrival of a baby in the household lead to your being ignored

- If you eat the carpet, make sure it's in a spot that can't easily be covered up

- Smile

- Fancy Lassie

When wet, don't shake until as many people as possible are within soaking distance

Don't eat grass – you'll make yourself sick

Wake a loved one with a lick

Only turn round and round before lying down if there's something there to flatten

Remember that playing with toilet paper is kid's stuff

Don't let on that you enjoyed it at the kennels

Make friends with the local butcher

Don't dig holes if you've nothing to put in them

- Learn to read 'No Dogs Allowed' signs – and ignore them

- Don't be the underdog

- Never fall over when cocking your leg

Don't walk to heel when you can be in front

Share your toys

Bark when strangers arrive at the house, not when they leave

- Remember, you're not a human being (who'd want to be?)

- Chase frisbees but not boomerangs

- Don't mate in public

If you want to be a successful gundog, don't eat the game

If you want to be a successful sheepdog, don't bite the sheep

Don't be humiliated – only enter a dog show if you have a chance of winning

Don't drink out of the toilet

Don't wolf down your food

Only challenge a burglar if:

    a) he's obviously harmless
    b) he's stealing *you*

 Never take a tablet unless it's administered inside a Mars bar

Don't be selfish – share your fleas

Don't eat spiders

Wear a seat belt

- Learn to shake hands

- Wear your collar and tag

- Prove your worth – don't be a dogsbody

If you're a mongrel, lie about your parentage

If you're a pedigree, deny any in-breeding

Know the difference between a hosepipe and a snake – you might get wet

Refrain from wagging your tail near fine china

Relish a good brushing

Refute the idea that one year counts for seven dog years once you get past ten

- Despise anyone who says you talk to them

- Know the sound of your master's car

- If you train as a police dog, don't expect every criminal to have padded arms

Always let people know the phone is ringing, even if they have perfect hearing

If you want a lucky star, choose Sirius – the Dog Star

Don't get too worried if some drunk asks for 'the hair of the dog'

- Be alert

- Have a sixth sense

- Keep your tail down when it's cold and windy

- Ignore playmates who tell you you're beginning to look like your owner

- Don't roll in dung

- Don't 'fetch' when you can eat it there

- Beware of passive smoking

- Don't walk into furniture if you have to wear a surgical collar

- If you become a sniffer dog, don't sniff too hard at the white powder

Cock your head on one side to show you're listening

Don't lie under the bird table and wonder why the birds don't come

Watch the sunset

Never *ever* be 'cute'

Look after your teeth

Never go to a pub without a garden

Don't whine

Don't lick your wounds

Don't eat toffees

Don't get fat

- Know when it's unwise to push your luck

- Rescue someone

- Treat dogs that are half your size with indifference

See *Lady and the Tramp*

Know the difference between relaxation and lethargy – and practise both

Don't chase your tail

Watch fish in ornamental fish ponds – but don't fall in

Don't fall for the 'Walkies' ploy to get you to come for your bath

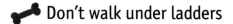 Don't walk under ladders

Don't steal liqueur chocolates if you suffer from hangovers

Know the sound of the ice cream van

If you hear someone say, 'I'll set the dog on you,' run and hide

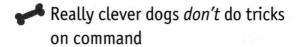 Really clever dogs *don't* do tricks on command

Remember, today's playful kitten is tomorrow's fierce cat

Only agree to being a guard dog if you can stay awake at night

Always stand up in the back of cars to obscure the driver's rear view

- Avoid children's parties

- One man's scraps is a hungry dog's feast

- Never let anyone call you a mongrel

Keep yourself clean – it's better than taking a bath

Don't hang your head, unless it's just a ruse to get your own way

- Lie in front of the fire, but not too close

- Don't pee up a houseplant

- Moult on dark carpets and car seats

Don't let your master take you for a walk as a cover for going out for a drink

Aspire to being the best of your breed, even if your owners are clearly not the best of theirs

Be proud of your private parts – don't be embarrassed about showing them off

Be nice to little boys – they'll grow up to be bigger than you

- Hide your tablet under your tongue for five minutes, then spit it out

- Lie somewhere warm when you're wet so you'll smell even stronger

Learn to spell so you'll recognize 'W-A-L-K' and 'F-O-O-D'

Never try to catch a ball that's small enough to swallow

- Don't easily be shifted from a comfy bed or chair without putting up a fight

- Don't try to mount the policeman's leg, even if uniforms do turn you on

- Eat snow, unless it's yellow

- Watch the tennis

- Never eat dogfood straight from the tin

- Don't get frisky towards smelly feet

- Ensure your owners boycott 'No Dogs' hotels

- Wander off during a long 'stay'

- Have a favourite armchair

- Enjoy solar heating – sleep in the greenhouse

- Own a 'Beware of the Dog' sign, regardless of temperament

- If someone tries to train you using the 'carrot and stick' method, eat the stick

- Never let a little rain dissuade you from taking a walk

Don't foul on the pavement unless it's next to a sign telling you not to

Remember, dogfood always looks meatier in the commercials

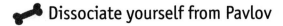 Dissociate yourself from Pavlov

Sulk

Sleep in a particularly dark spot on the stairs

Never be fooled into mistaking a human pretending to bark for the real thing

Insist on commands directed at you being prefaced by 'Please'

Only chew up *important* mail

Require a minimum of 23 hours' rest a day

Always take the shortest route

See an analyst

Two of life's great mysteries are:

a) If little boys do have puppy dogs' tails, have they been docked?

b) If it's a dog's life, why is life a bitch?

 Live in hope